THE NEW COLLECTOR'S

By Barr

Fourth Edition

Revised September 2017

Table of Contents

Preface

As with any specialized field, pocket watch collecting has its own terminology, and it is not always easy for the novice collector to understand what the "experts" are talking about. What does it mean to say that a watch has "jewels" or that it is "adjusted"? What is a "hunter case" watch? What's the difference between a railroad "grade" watch and a railroad "approved" watch? What is a "lever set" watch? Isn't "rolled gold" a brand of pretzel?

Many people are fascinated by pocket watches, but are a bit intimidated by the thought of actually owning a miniaturized piece of complicated machinery made a hundred years ago [or more]. Collecting old pocket watches can be an extremely fun and rewarding hobby, but it can also be a bit frustrating at first if you don't understand what it is that you've actually got.

When I first started collecting pocket watches years ago, I knew absolutely nothing about them except that they looked nice and I wanted one. In fact, I couldn't even figure out how to set the time on my first watch [I thought it must be broken, and almost **did** break it trying to set it the wrong way!] The books I looked at were certainly useful and full of great information, but they all seemed to be written with the assumption that I already knew what they were talking about. What I really needed was somebody I could just ask a bunch of really basic questions, and who wouldn't make fun of me no matter **how** dumb the question.

Well, this booklet is full of all the things I wish somebody had told me when I first started collecting, and which I have shared with many new collectors over the years. Keep in mind that I have tried to keep things as simple and basic as possible for quick and easy comprehension, which necessarily means that this is **not** a scholarly treatise. But hopefully this will give you enough information to get you started and also give you a clue what those "other" books are talking about.

Chapter 1. A Brief History of Timekeeping

For much of human history, precise timekeeping simply wasn't that big of a deal. Aside from the fact that there wasn't any way to keep accurate time thousands of years ago, there simply wasn't the need to do so. Early cultures that were based on agriculture worked as long as the sun shone and stopped when it got dark. It was only as Mankind began to move away from a purely agrarian society that people began to look for a way to mark the passage of time more precisely than simply dividing each day into "day" and "night."

The earliest known device to break the day down into smaller chunks of time was the **sundial**, which was invented at least by 1500 B.C. Having noticed that the shadow which an object casts changes in length and direction as the day progresses, some bright person whose name shall be forever lost to history realized that you could place a stick upright in the ground and, by marking where the shadow fell, divide the daylight into discrete intervals. These intervals eventually came to be called "hours," with each hour being 1/12th of the time the sun shone each day. The sundial was a wonderful idea that allowed for the orderly progression of the ancient Greek and Roman civilizations. One great thing about the sundial was that it was very portable. It did have some very basic flaws, however. First and foremost, it only worked when the sun was actually shining. This wasn't a problem at night, since nobody worked in the dark anyway. But it *was* a major problem on cloudy days. Even when the sun was brightly shining, however, the length of the day varies throughout the course of the year, which meant that the length of an "hour" also varied by as much as 30 minutes from the Summer solstice to the Winter solstice.

Because of the limitations of the sundial, people looked for other ways to measure the passage of time without being dependent on the sun. One of the early attempts that became very popular was the **water clock** [also called the **clepsydra**], invented sometime around 1000 B.C. The water clock was based on the idea that water leaks out of a small hole at an apparently steady rate, and it is possible to mark the passage of time by noting how much water has leaked out through a hole in the bottom of a specially marked vessel. Water clocks were much more accurate than sundials, since the rate of flow was unaffected by the time of day or year, and it didn't matter whether the sun was shining or not. They were not without their own serious flaws, though.

Although water may *appear* to drip at a steady, fixed rate, in fact the more water is in the vessel the faster it leaks out due to the pressure exerted by the weight of the water. The ancient Egyptians solved this problem by using vessels with slanted sides to equalize the water pressure as the amount of water decreased. Other problems, however, included the fact that the hole through which the water dripped tended to get larger over time, thereby permitting more water to pass through quicker, and the fact that the escape hole also had a nasty tendency to get clogged. And heaven forbid it should get cold enough for the water to actually freeze! Water clocks, by their very nature, were also not particularly portable.

Well, it didn't take people long to realize that water isn't the only thing that flows at a steady pace, and next up came the **hourglass**, invented sometime around the 8th century A.D. The main reason it wasn't invented earlier was probably simply because nobody was able to blow glass well enough before then. The hourglass uses sand flowing from one glass vessel into another through a tiny opening which connects the two, and the passage of the sand is not particularly affected by the things which caused problems with the water clock and the sundial before it. However, large hourglasses were impractical, and keeping time for any extended period usually meant turning the glass over and over again over the course of a day. Basically, it made a great *timer*, but a lousy *timekeeper*.

And that's pretty much how things stood until the 1300's, when a bunch of monks in Europe decided they really needed a better way to tell when it was time to pray. For, you see, a monk's life revolved around a set schedule of prayers – one at first light, one at sunrise, one at mid-morning, one at noon, one at mid- afternoon, one at sunset and one at nightfall. Knowing the correct time therefore became more than just a nicety – it was a religious imperative! And, as a result, these monks devised the first known mechanical **clocks**. The word "clock," by the way, comes from the Dutch word for "bell," since these early mechanical clocks had no hands and were designed to simply strike the hour.

In addition to the bell striking mechanism, these early clocks had two important requirements. The first was a source of power, and this was provided by a weight attached to a rope or chain. The weight was carried or pulled to the top of the clock, and gravity would do the rest. The second was some way to force the weight to fall in a slow, measured pace instead of plummeting like, well, a lead weight. And this was provided by a wonderful and ingenious invention called the **escapement**. In simplest terms, an escapement is a device that interrupts the path of the falling weight at regular intervals, causing it to fall a little bit at a time instead of all at once. This is literally what makes clocks "tick," since as the escapement moves back and forth, alternately engaging and releasing the gears that are attached to the weight, it makes a very distinctive sound.

These earliest clocks, while technological marvels, were not particularly accurate. Also, while they allowed the hour to be subdivided into more minute portions [hence our word "minute" for the first small division of the hour], they could not break the hour down into a further, or "second" small division [and yes, that's where *that* word comes from as well]. That had to wait until a rather brilliant young man named Galileo Galilei discovered the principal of the **pendulum** in about 1583. Stated broadly, he noticed that regardless of how wide a particular pendulum swung, it always took the same amount of time to swing back and forth. He discovered, in fact, that the amount of time it took the pendulum to return was determined by the length of the pendulum itself and not by the width of the swing. And, by attaching a precisely measured pendulum to a clock's escapement, clockmakers were able to produce timepieces that were accurate to within seconds per day instead of minutes. It didn't matter how much force was applied to the pendulum, since the force only affected the width of the swing and not the length of the pendulum itself.

So now we had timepieces that worked well no matter the time of day or season, and which were very accurate over long periods of time. Unfortunately, they still weren't particularly portable, due to the fact that the weight wouldn't fall regularly and the pendulum couldn't work correctly if they were subjected to outside motion. And this is where the pocket watch enters the picture.

The key invention that allowed clocks to become portable [and what is a watch but a portable clock?] was the **spring**. In fact, the use of springs is probably the second most important horological development after the invention of the escapement. The first step in making a clock portable was to replace the heavy weights used to power it with something that would exert a steady force regardless of the position in which the clock was held. And it was discovered that a tightly coiled, high-tension strip of metal exerts a more or less steady force as it uncoils, which made it just the thing for the job. Of course, it didn't take long for clockmakers to notice that the spring exerted less and less force as it unwound, but they came up with a number of rather ingenious ways to deal with the problem, including such devices as the "stackfreed" and the "fusee."

The second step in making a clock truly portable was coming up with a replacement for the pendulum which kept the clock ticking at precisely timed intervals. Early "portable clocks" used a device called a "foliot," which consisted of two very small weights suspended from either end of a rotating balance bar, but these were neither particularly accurate nor truly portable. Once again, however, it was the newly discovered concept of the spring that came to the rescue. It was determined that a very fine coil of wire [called a "hairspring" since it was so thin] could be attached directly to the balance wheel, and that when force from the main spring was transmitted to the escapement, the attached hairspring would coil and uncoil at a very regular pace, thereby causing the escapement to engage and release in the required precisely timed intervals. And, for the most part, this is true no matter how the clock is held, providing true portability.

The distinction between these first early portable clocks and the first true pocket watches is a blurry one. Although a spring-driven clock may have been developed as early as the 1400's, a spring *regulated* clock did not appear until the mid 1600's, and it wasn't long after that before they became small enough to carry on one's waist or in one's pocket. And soon, anybody who could afford one was seen carrying that newfangled invention that was all the rage – the pocket watch.

Chapter 2.   Basic Terminology

Just so we are all on the same page, here are some basic terms that are commonly used among watch collectors and which I use in this booklet. Terms that require a longer explanation have their own entry later on in the booklet.

Arbor – Another name for the shaft that passes through each of the gears, or **wheels**, that make up the bulk of a watch's **movement**. The arbor of the **balance wheel** is called the "balance staff." The tip of the arbor is called the "**pivot**."

Balance Wheel – The little wheel visible on most watch **movements** that rotates rapidly back and forth. The balance serves the same purpose as the pendulum in a clock. Balance wheels on older [pre-20th Century] watches are usually flat steel or gold, while on later watches they usually have a number of small screws attached that are used to adjust the watch for accuracy.

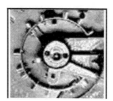

Figure 1: The Balance Wheel

Bezel – The ring of metal that holds the **crystal** in place. Bezels can usually be removed by either prying them off or unscrewing them, depending on the watch, but care should be taken not to break the crystal in the process.

Bridge – the **movement** of a watch consists of a top and bottom plate of metal, between which are located all the gears. On many watches the top plate of the watch [the plate visible when you remove the back cover] is divided into separate sections, called "bridges." A "two finger bridge" or a "three-finger bridge" watch is one that has two or three short narrow bridges next to each other that resemble fingers. The **balance wheel** usually has its own separate bridge that is often referred to as the "balance bridge" [or the "balance cock," especially on older watches].

Figure 2: Three Examples of Bridges

Case – The metal shell that houses the actual **movement** of the watch. Cases can be made of gold, silver, brass, nickel or a variety of other metals. Some are plain, whereas others are extremely ornate. Many collectors are more interested in the movement than the case, but there are also those who prize a good case above all else. And, of course, a great movement in a great case makes **everybody** happy!

Figure 3: The Case

Chronograph – With American watches, a chronograph is a combination watch and stopwatch. With English watches, the term is often used to denote a watch that can be stopped and restarted on demand for timing or calibration purposes. Most chronographs are easily recognizable by the fact that they have a central sweep second hand, and many also have separate small dials [or "registers"] to keep track of elapsed time.

Chronometer – Denotes a watch of superior quality. Note that just **calling** a watch a chronometer doesn't necessarily make it one. This term is also used to refer to watches with a chronometer-style **escapement**.

Crown – The knob attached to the top of the **winding stem**.

Figure 4: The Crown

Crystal – The transparent covering over the **dial** that protects it from dust and damage. Crystals can be either glass [called "mineral crystals"] or plastic [called "acrylic crystals"]. And yes, I realize that "plastic crystal" is an oxymoron, but hey – I didn't come up with the term! Plastic crystals have been around since the 1930's, and the earliest ones were actually made of celluloid. Remaining examples of celluloid crystals are often discolored with age. In general, plastic crystals tend to scratch more easily than mineral crystals. On the bright side, though, they don't tend to break as easily as mineral ones.

Damaskeening [also spelled "damascening"] – A wholly American idiom [probably a corruption of "Damascus"] used to describe the detailed engraving many watch companies put on their **movements**. Damaskeening comes in many different patterns, and is an art form in its own right.

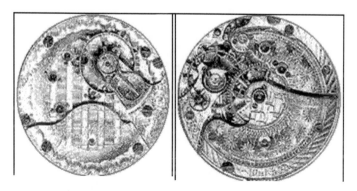

Figure 5: Two Examples of Finely Damaskeened Watch Movements

Demi-Hunter Case [also known as a "half-hunter" case] – This is a **hunter case** that has a circular window cut out of the front cover, often with an additional **crystal** inset. Most demi-hunter cases have additional numbers on front cover of the case that correspond to the numbers on the **dial**, which means that you can actually tell the time by looking through the central window without having to actually open the case. A "true" demi-hunter cased watch will also have a special hour hand with an additional pointer on it that can be seen with the cover closed.

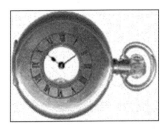 

Figure 6: Demi-Hunter Case   Figure 7: Special Hour Hand

Dial – The face of the watch, often made of enamel over metal or just metal, where the numbers and hands are located. Clocks have faces. Watches have dials.

Dust Cover [also known as a "cuvette"] – An inner cover protecting the **movement** of the watch from the harmful effects of the environment. This is most often found with **hunter case** watches.

Figure 8: The Dust Cover

Ebauche – In general, this refers to a style of watch **movement** that was mass produced by various Swiss companies in the mid to late 1800's and which were then shipped to retailers or jewelers who "finished" the watch by adding the **dial**, hands, **case**, jewels, the **escapement**, etc. Quite often the name engraved on a European watch from this period is that of the retailer and not of the company that actually made the watch itself.

Figure 9: An Ebauche from the Early 1800's

Figure 10: An Ebauche from the Early to Mid 1800's

Figure 11: An Ebauche from the Mid to Late 1800's

Figure 12: An Ebauche from the Late 1800's to Early 1900's

Escapement – Left to its own devices, the **mainspring** of a watch would wind down in a matter of seconds. The escapement is the part of the watch mechanism that keeps this from happening, forcing the mainspring to instead unwind at a slow, regular pace. The regular interaction between the parts of the escapement is what produces the distinctive "ticking" sound. There are numerous types of escapements found in different watches, including the "verge" escapement, the "lever" escapement and the "cylinder" escapement, and all do the same job but in slightly different ways. The verge escapement is an early form of escapement that is usually not particularly accurate. This was followed by the cylinder escapement that was more accurate, but still usually not great. The lever escapement, although invented in the 1760's, did not come into wide use until the mid to late 1800's and was much more reliable than its predecessors.

Hairspring – An incredibly fine and delicate metal coil attached to the balance wheel that expands and contracts and thus allows the **balance**

wheel to rotate back and forth as it receives power from the mainspring. This serves the same function as a pendulum in a clock. If the hairspring is attached to bottom of the balance wheel, the watch is referred to as being "**under sprung**."

 **The Hairspring**

Figure 13: The Hairspring

Hunter Case [also known as "hunting case"] – A "hunter case" watch is simply a watch with a front cover. A watch without a front cover is called an open face watch. To open a hunter case watch and tell the time, hold the watch with the crown [the knob that sticks out of the top of the watch] facing the right, and then push the crown in with your thumb. If the "lift spring" is in good working condition, the front cover should pop open. If not, you may need to pry it open with your thumbnail. When closing a hunter case watch be sure to press the crown in to keep the little "catch" from wearing.

Mainspring – A long, thin strip of highly tensile metal which is coiled up inside the watch mechanism and which gives the watch it's power. Winding a watch coils the spring, and it slowly unwinds over the course of the day. The mainspring replaces the heavy weights which were previously used in clocks and which depended on gravity. The mainspring is housed within the "**Mainspring Barrel**" which slowly rotates as the spring unwinds.

Movement – The inner workings of the watch, the "guts" or "works." The actual watch itself, as opposed to the **case** which may or may not be original to the watch. When a collector refers to a watch's serial number, he or she is talking about the number engraved on the movement. The movement will also frequently have the name of the watch company and other information such as the number of **jewels**, whether it is adjusted, etc. You don't need to disassemble a watch to view the movement -- opening the back cover will usually do the trick

Figure 14: Three Examples of Different Watch Movements

Pinion – The smaller, solid gears of a watch. A "Saftey Pinion" was a special design used on many watches to reduce the risk of damage to the movement in the event the mainspring should break.

Pivot – Most **wheels** are held in place by an **arbor** which passes through the center of the wheel and which connects to the upper and lower plates of the movement. The pivot is the tip of the arbor that actually fits into the hole in the plate and which is surrounded by a **jewel** if the wheel in question is jeweled.

Regulator – A device near the **balance wheel** that allows you speed up or slow down the watch to a small degree. Most American watches have regulators marked "**F**" ["fast"] and "**S**" ["slow"], whereas many European watches are marked "**A**" ["advance"] and "**R**" ["retard"]. Some regulators have a simple needle that can be pushed in the desired direction. Other regulators [especially those found on higher grade watches] are designed so that they can be moved only a little bit at a time for precise calibration, and these are generally referred to as **micrometric regulators**. Adjusting a micrometric regulator may require special tools, so when in doubt bring it to an expert.

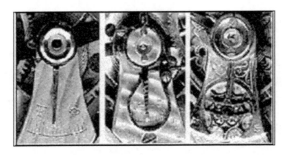

Figure 15: Three Examples of Different Regulators

Sidewinder – Hunter case watches were designed so that the winding stem was at the 3:00 position. Frequently, however, a watch that was designed for a hunter case ends up being recased into an open face case somewhere along the line. The result is an open face watch that still has its winding stem at the 3:00 position instead of 12:00. Because these watches wind at the side of the watch instead of the top, they are often referred to as "sidewinder" watches. Whenever you see a sidewinder, keep in mind that it probably did not start out life looking like that. Note also that some sidewinders have been retrofitted with special "conversion" dials that have the small dial for the second hands located at the 3:00 position instead of the 6:00, which allows them to have the winding stem in the proper 12:00 position. These may seem strange or exotic to the new collector, but keep in mind that – once again – this probably isn't how they started out.

Stem [also referred to as the "pendant"] – The shaft that sticks out of the watch. Technically, the stem is the actual shaft and the pendant is the outer casing, but the terms are often interchanged. On watches that are "stem wind," you turn the crown on top of the stem to wind them, and on watches that are "pendant set," you pull out the crown and turn it to set the time. The stem usually has a loop of metal above it [the "bow"] that can be used to attach a carrying chain.

Figure 16: The Winding Stem

Wheel – The larger [usually spoked] gears of a watch are called "wheels". Most wheels have a smaller, solid gear that sits on top or below it, and which meshes with other wheels, and these are called "pinions."

Chapter 3.   Parts of a Pocket Watch Movement

The following diagram illustrates the main parts of a standard American pocket watch movement with a **lever escapement**. Note that the exact design and arrangement of each part varies from company to company and from model to model.

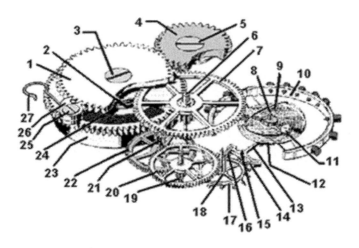

1.	Ratchet/Winding Wheel		15.	Pallet Arbor
2.	Barrel Arbor		16.	Pallet Jewel
3.	Ratchet/Winding Wheel Screw		17.	Escape Wheel
4.	Crown/Main Wheel		18.	Escape Pinion
5.	Crown/Main Wheel Screw		19.	Fourth Pinion
6.	Center Pinion		20.	Fourth Wheel
7.	Center Wheel		21.	Third Pinion
8.	Balance Staff		22.	Third Wheel
9.	Hairspring		23.	Mainspring Barrel/First Wheel
10.	Balance Wheel		24.	Mainspring
11.	Hairspring Stud		25.	Click Screw
12.	Fork		26.	Winding Click
13.	Lever		27.	Click Spring
14.	Pallet Jewel			

Chapter 4.   What's the Difference Between Grade and Model?

The **model** of a watch is the **overall design** of the watch's movement. In general, the model defines the size and shape of the plates and/or bridges. The model especially defines the layout of the (gear) train and the design of the vast majority of the parts. Waltham watches have model numbers which roughly correspond to the first year they were produced [1883, 1892, 1912, etc.] Other companies used names such as "Series 1," "Model #2," etc.

If the model of a watch denotes the general design of the movement, the **grade** refers to variations between examples of the same model. These variations can include such things as the number of jewels, how well-finished the movement is, whether the movement has screw-down jewel settings, etc. Sometimes these variations can be significant, and a particular model can come in a variety of grades from low quality to high. Often, however, the term "grade" is used merely to distinguish between minor variations, and in some cases two different grades are actually identical except for the name. Grades were frequently named after individuals who worked at the watch company, famous historical figures, railroad lines, previous names of the company, and just about anything else you can think of. Thus, you might have a Waltham Model #1892, "Vanguard" grade. Or an Illinois Series 6 "Bunn Special."

Keep in mind that "model" and "grade" are technical definitions and are often used interchangeably. Some watch companies used the term "grade" almost exclusively without distinguishing between different Models. Other companies used the same grade name with more than one model. So, for example, it is important to distinguish between a Waltham Model #1857 "P. S. Bartlett" grade and a Model #1883 "P. S. Bartlett" grade, since they are completely different watches. The Hamilton "992" grade, on the other hand, was only made in one basic model and is just referred to as the Hamilton 992.

Chapter 5. How Are Different Watches Set?

Most people think that you set a pocket watch the same way you set a wristwatch -- by pulling out the winding stem. Well, that *is* true with many pocket watches, but by no means all of them! In fact, there are four main ways pocket watches can be set, and if you don't know how your watch is set you can break it by pulling too hard on the stem.

Stem Set [also called "pendant set"]. You probably already know this one -- you pull on the crown on top of the stem and turn it to set the time. If you pull on the crown and it doesn't move, chances are your watch is not stem set.

Lever Set. Often found in American-made railroad grade watches, but also in other watches, the lever setting mechanism requires you to pull out a little lever [a thin sliver of metal usually found near the 2:00 or 4:00 position]. You then turn the stem to move the hands. This was a safety feature to prevent the watch from being accidentally reset when someone pulled on the stem. On **hunter case** watch, the lever should be visible simply by opening the front cover. On an open face watch, however, you normally have to remove the front **bezel** to expose the lever. Be VERY careful when doing this, as it is all too easy to damage the crystal and/or the dial in the process.

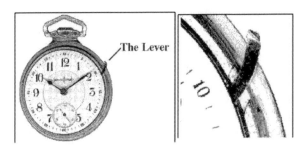

Figure 17: Lever Set

Pin Set. Also called "nail set," this involves a little button found on the case to the immediate left or right of the **stem** that must be pushed and held while the stem is turned. This served the same feature as the lever set mechanism, but is usually found on European pocket watches.

Figure 18: Pin Set

Key Set. If you need a key to wind your watch, chances are you need a key to set it as well. Usually a single key is used to wind and set a given watch, but not always. Some key wind watches have two holes in the back, one to wind and one to set, and the setting hole is the one in the very center. Other key wind watches, however, are set from the front, requiring you to remove the **bezel** and place the key directly on the central shaft that runs through the hour and minute hands.

Chapter 6.   How Do You Open the Back of a Watch?

Most of the information crucial to identifying a particular pocket watch is inscribed on the watch **movement**. Different watches allow you to see the movement in different ways, however, and if you don't realize how your watch opens up you can damage it.

Pry Off – on many watches the back cover simply pries open. Sometimes there is an inner "dust" cover that must also be pried open to expose the movement. Often, you will be able to see a hinge on the back, which indicates that the cover opens this way, but occasionally the cover will just pop off. You can usually pry off the cover with a thumbnail or a dull knife blade, but if you are having difficulty make sure that the cover really **does** pry off before you break something! Also, if you decide to use something sharp like a razorblade or Swiss army knife, be **very** careful you don't slice your thumb in the process. Also, care should be taken not to scratch the case. If the cover is meant to be pried off, there will often be a small indentation or "lip" where the blade or thumbnail can be inserted, and if you can't find any sign of a lip, it may not be a pry off cover. . .

Screw Off – Surprise! Some back covers simply screw off, a fact I learned after unsuccessfully trying to pry off the back cover on one of my first watches. If you can't pry the cover off, try unscrewing it in a counter-clockwise direction. Just be careful you don't grip the front of the watch so tightly that you end up breaking the **crystal** in the process. If you have any doubt whether a cover is pry off or screw off, by the way, it is always safer to try screwing it off first. You're less likely to damage a pry off cover by trying to unscrew it than you are to damage a screw off cover by trying to pry it off.

Swing Out -- Some watches don't actually **have** a back cover, or else the back cover only exposes the inner **dust cover** and not the **movement**. These are usually swing out cases that open from the **front**. To open a swing out case, you first need to open the front **bezel** [it's usually hinged and pries off or else needs to be unscrewed]. If it's a stem wind watch, you will then probably need to carefully pull on the **winding stem** until you hear a soft click. The movement should then swing out from the bottom, while remaining attached to the case via a hinge at the top. Care should be taken to not pull too hard, since you don't want to actually pull the stem right out of the case. And if the stem doesn't pull out with gentle pressure, make sure that the watch isn't really in a pry off or screw off case before pulling any harder.

If it's a key wind watch, instead of pulling on the stem you will probably need to press in a tiny catch at the base of the dial near the 6. This can be a bit of a delicate procedure, and if you have any doubts about whether this is really a swing out case or not your best bet is to bring it to somebody a bit more knowledgeable.

Chapter 7.   What Size Is My Watch?

When a collector refers to an American watch's "size," he or she is generally referring to the diameter of the watch **movement** only, not the case. The same size watch movement will usually fit in a variety of different size cases, so the size of the case is usually not helpful in identifying the watch.

European watches are typically referred to by their size in millimeters. A small ladies' watch might be 30 or 35mm, whereas a men's watch could be upwards of 50 or 60mm.

American watches, on the other hand, have their own special sizing scale. Most American watches fall between 0 and 18 size, with 0 being the smallest and 18 being the largest. The most common sizes are 18, 16 and 12 for men's watches, and 8, 6 and 0 for ladies' watches. The size 10 watch is right in the middle and is generally considered to be either a men's or a ladies' watch.

The following table shows the standard American watch movement sizes and their equivalent size in inches:

Watch Size	Size in Inches
18	1 23/30 [1.8]
16	1 21/30 [1.7]
12	1 17/30 [1.566]
10	1 ½ [1.5]
8	1 13/30 [1.433]
6	1 11/30 [1.366]
0	1 5/30 [1.166]

As you might expect, it can be a bit tricky measuring a watch movement to determine its size, not only because many of the sizes are so close to each other, but also because it's not that easy to measure such odd sizes in the first place. Also, the sizing chart above refers to the size of the plate **under the dial** [which may or may not be the same diameter as the dial itself], and on some watches that plate has a slightly different diameter than the plate visible when simply viewing the movement. Experienced collectors, however, can often tell the size of most watches simply by looking at the movement and comparing it to other, similar, watches they have seen before. As with any skill, this ability comes primarily through experience, but here are some quick pointers when dealing with American watches:

With many American watch companies, the movements of different size watches look completely different from other sizes made by the same company. Therefore, once you learn to recognize a particular size and model you can usually use that knowledge to identify similar watches.

Most **18 size** American watches were made with "full plate" movements. This means that when you open the back of the watch you can't see any of the inner workings of the watch movement – just the **balance wheel** and perhaps the winding wheels [the wheels that turn when you wind the watch], as shown in the following examples:

Figure 19: An 18 Size Illinois "Bunn Special"

Figure 20: An 18 Size Waltham "Vanguard"

Most smaller watches, on the other hand, have movements where the top plate is divided into two or more "**bridges**." On these watches it is usually possible to see into the inner workings of the movement to some degree and one or more gears can often be seen, as shown in the following examples. Note that watch movements where the bridges cover most, but not all, of the inner workings are frequently referred to as "3/4 plate" movements.

Figure 21: A 16 Size Waltham "Vanguard" Figure 22: A 16 Size Illinois "Bunn Special"

Earlier American watches from the 1800's were most often **18 size**, whereas **16 size** watches became popular for men after the turn of the century. By the 1920's **12 size** watches became very popular for men as well.

Until the early 1900's, railroad grade watches could be either 18 size or 16 size. By the 1930's however, most railroad watches were 16 size, and this later became a requirement for railroad watches.

Chapter 8.   What Are Watch "Jewels"?

A watch **movement** mostly consists of a number of gears [called "**wheels**"] held in place by an upper and a lower plate. Each wheel has a central shaft [called an "**arbor**"] running through it, the ends of which fit into holes in the plates. If you have a metal shaft in a metal hole, with nothing to protect it, it will eventually wear away as the shaft turns. To prevent wear, and also to reduce friction, most watches have tiny doughnut-shaped jewels at the ends of many of the wheel arbors to keep them from coming into direct contact with the edges of the hole. The jewels are usually natural or man-made rubies, but can also be diamonds and sapphires. The fastest moving wheels [especially the **balance wheel**] on a watch frequently have additional "cap" jewels on top of the regular "hole" jewels to prevent the arbor from moving up and down, and most watches also have a few special jewels [called "pallet" and "roller" jewels] as part of the **escapement**.

Very early pocket watches rarely had jewels, simply because the concept hadn't been invented yet or wasn't in common use. By the mid 1800's, watches typically had 6-10 jewels, and a watch with 15 jewels was considered high grade.

By the 20th century, however, more and more watches were being made with higher jewel counts, and the quality of a watch is often judged by how many jewels it has. Thus, lower grade American-made watches from the late 1800's and into the 1900's typically have jewels only on the **balance wheel** and the **escapement** [7 jewels total]. Medium grade watches have 11-17 jewels, and high grade watches usually have 19-21 jewels. Extremely complicated watches, such as chronometers, chronographs, calendar and chiming watches, might have upwards of 32 jewels, and some high grade railroad watches have "cap" jewels on the slower wheels in addition to the faster moving wheels.

Note that, although the number of jewels that a watch has is usually a good indication as to its overall quality, this is not an absolute standard for three main reasons. First, as mentioned above, many watches made prior to the 20th century were considered to be "high grade" for their day, in spite of the fact that they only have 15 jewels. Second, some watches have extra jewels that were added primarily for show and which did not add to the watch's accuracy or quality [and which were sometimes not even real jewels to begin with!] Third, there has been significant debate over the years as to how many jewels a watch even needs to be considered "high grade." Webb C. Ball, the man most responsible for setting the standards by which railroad watches were judged in the late 1800's and early 1900's, claimed that anything beyond 17 or 19 jewels was not only unnecessary, but actually made a watch more difficult to maintain and repair. The more common notion of "the more jewels the better" is not likely to go away anytime soon, however.

Most pocket watches made in the late 1800's and thereafter that have more than 15 jewels have the jewel count marked directly on the **movement**. If there is no jewel count marked, and the only visible jewels are the ones on the balance staff [right in the center of the **balance wheel**], the watch probably only has 7 jewels. Note that a watch with 11 jewels looks identical to one with 15 jewels, since the extra 4 jewels are on the side of the movement directly under the dial. Also, a 17 jewel watch looks the same as a 21 jewel watch to the naked eye, since the additional jewels in this case are usually all cap jewels at the top and bottom of two of the wheels.

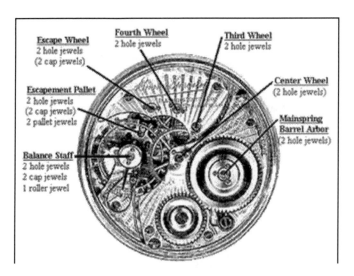

Figure 23: Location of the jewels on a 16 size, 23 jewel Illinois "Bunn Special."

(Jewels in parentheses are typically found only on higher grade watches. The exact arrangement of jewels varied from company to company.)

Chapter 9.   What Does "Adjusted" Mean?

Many pocket watches state that they are "adjusted" to temperature and to a number of positions. This basically means that they have been specially calibrated to maintain the same accuracy under a variety of conditions. A watch that has been adjusted to temperature will keep the same time regardless of temperature. A watch that has been adjusted to position will keep the same time regardless of how it is held. There are six possible position adjustments: stem up, stem down, stem left, stem right, dial up and dial down. Most railroad grade watches are adjusted to five positions [they didn't bother with stem down, since few people keep their watches upside down in their pockets]. Most watches that are adjusted are also adjusted to "isochronism," meaning that they keep the same time as the mainspring winds down.

Almost all watches made in the 20th century are adjusted to temperature and isochronism, and this is frequently not mentioned on the watch anywhere [although some high grade watches will say something like "adjusted to temperature and 5 positions"]. Occasionally, you will see a watch marked "8 adjustments," but this simply means that the watch either is adjusted to five positions, as well as to heat, cold and isochronism, or it is adjusted to six positions, temperature (another way of saying heat and cold) and isochronism. A watch that is simply marked "adjusted" may be adjusted to several positions, but could also simply be adjusted to temperature and isochronism.

Chapter 10.   Railroad Watches

Many collectors feel that American watchmaking reached its pinnacle with the invention of the railroad watch. In an effort to meet the stringent and rigorous demands of the railroads, where the incorrect time could and did prove disastrous, American watchmakers were called upon to make a watch that was incredibly reliable and incredibly accurate -- far more so than any watch previously being manufactured. And they met the challenge! Following years of development, by the turn of the 20th century American watch factories were producing pocket watches of unsurpassed quality. Watches that would lose no more than 30 seconds per week. Watches that were specially adjusted to keep accurate time no matter what position in which they were held, and in both cold weather and hot. Watches where all the major **wheels** were jeweled in order to prevent wear from long hours, days, years and decades of constant use.

The main requirement for a railroad watch was, of course, that it be accurate. Throughout the twenty years from 1890 to 1910, the various railroads' watch standards evolved, demanding more stringent adherence to safety and good timekeeping principles. Although minor local differences remained, these standards eventually became well enough established and accepted so that watch companies could build, at reasonable cost, both 18 size, and later 16 size, watches that would be accepted on any railroad. The standards continued to evolve, and by the 1930's, only size 16 watches were approved, and these watches had to also have at least 19 jewels, be **lever set**, open face and **adjusted** to five positions, temperature and isochronism. Some railroads, however, continued to accept watches that were currently in use and which had previously been approved under earlier standards.

Not all watches that were built to meet the railroad standards were actually accepted for service on all railroads. Many railroads published their own lists of "approved" watches, and these lists varied from one railroad to the next. Thus, it is possible to have a railroad "grade" watch that was never actually railroad "approved." Even if a watch wasn't specifically listed as "approved" for a particular railroad, however, there were also instances where a particular watch was accepted for service by the inspector out in the field and would thus still be considered "railroad approved."

The official railroad standards were only the **minimum** standards that a railroad grade watch had to meet, and many pocket watches that were approved for railroad service were actually made to **higher** specifications than required for a "railroad grade" watch. Many companies produced extra fine railroad watches that had 21-23 jewels [sometimes more!] that were adjusted to six positions instead of just five, and even had extra "wind indicator" dials to let you know how much the watch was currently wound. These watches are especially prized by many collectors as being the absolute best of the best.

Figure 24: A Wind Indicator

Remember, just because a watch has a picture of a locomotive on the dial or the case doesn't mean it is actually a "railroad" watch. The same is true with watches that are just marked "railroad special" or the like. A true railroad grade watch MUST meet the specifications set out for railroad watches, and a true railroad approved watch MUST have been either listed by one or more railroads as approved for railroad service or else specifically accepted by a railroad inspector. Some of the more commonly found railroad grade and approved watches include the Hamilton "992," the Illinois "Bunn Special" and the Waltham "Vanguard," although there are quite a few more out there. If you are considering paying a lot for a "railroad" watch, though, just be sure you're getting what you are paying for.

Figure 25: A 16 Size Waltham "Vanguard"

Figure 26: A 16 size Hamilton "992"

Figure 27: A 16 size Illinois "Bunn Special"

Chapter 11.   What is a "Fusee"?

Early clocks were powered by heavy weights attached to long chains. Every day the weight was returned to the top of the clock, and throughout the day gravity pulled the weight down, thereby causing the gears to move. Unfortunately, this only worked if the clock was mounted vertically and there was room for the weights to hang down. The invention of the mainspring, though, enabled clocks to be portable and eventually gave rise to what we call a pocket watch today. One problem with early mainsprings, though, was that as the spring wound down it lost power, and as a result the watch or clock would get slower and slower as the day progressed.

"Fusee" [also called "chain driven"] watches use a very fine chain running from the mainspring barrel to a special truncated cone [the "fusee"] to regulate the force of the spring as it winds down, as shown in the examples below:

Figure 28: The Fusee   Figure 29: The Mainspring Barrel

As the mainspring unwinds, the chain moves from the top of the fusee to the bottom, thereby increasing the tension on the mainspring. The older fusee watches used a "verge" **escapement** that, because it is mounted vertically within the watch, required the watch to be very thick. These watches, generally referred to as "verge fusees," were usually not as accurate as their later counterparts, although there were some notable exceptions such as John Harrison's famous "No. 4" marine chronometer. Perhaps to make up for this lack of accuracy, verge fusees were almost always works of art, employing intricately engraved and hand pierced balance **bridges** [or "cocks"] and other ornamentations.

In the early 1800's fusee watches began to be made with the newer "lever" escapement which, because they were mounted horizontally instead of vertically, allowed the watches to be thinner. These so-called "lever fusees" were also generally much more accurate as well. As the watches became more accurate timekeepers, however, less emphasis was placed on making them as artistic, and you rarely see much in the way of hand piercing or engraving on the later lever fusee watches.

Figure 30: A Verge Fusee Watch from 1776.

(Note the Ornately Hand- Pierced Balance Cock)

Figure 31: A Lever Fusee Watch from about 1887.

(More Accurate, But Not as Beautiful.)

Improved mainspring design, as well as special adjustments to the **balance wheel** and **hairspring**, eventually did away with the need for the fusee. By about 1850 most American watchmakers had abandoned the fusee entirely, although many English watchmakers continued to make fusee watches right up until the beginning of the 20th century. One notable exception was the American Hamilton Watch Company that decided to use a fusee in their Model #21 Marine Chronometer that they built for the U.S. Government in the 1940's. This was probably due more to the fact that they built their model based upon existing European designed chronometers, though, than it had to do with the need for the special properties of the fusee.

One important note about winding a fusee watch: although many French and Swiss fusees are wound through a hole in the dial, most English fusees are wound from the back like a "normal" key wind watch. There is one very important difference, though! A "normal" [i.e., non fusee] watch winds in a clockwise direction. The same is true for most fusee watches that wind through a hole in the dial. A fusee that is wound from the back, however, winds in a **COUNTER CLOCKWISE** direction. Because the fusee chain is so delicate, it is all too easy to break it if you try to wind the watch in the wrong direction. So, if you have any doubt as to whether your watch is a fusee or not, be sure to try gently winding it in a counter clockwise direction first!

One final tidbit of information: fusee watches are distinctive not only for the fusee itself but also for the fine chain running from the fusee to the special mainspring barrel. A non-fusee watch is therefore generally referred to as having a "**going barrel**" to distinguish it from a fusee watch.

Chapter 12.   What Do those Funny Words on My Watch Mean?

Many European-made pocket watches have a wealth of information written on the **dust cover** and/or **movement**. Unfortunately, not only are the words often in a foreign language such as French, they are often highly idiomatic and not in common usage today. Many novice collectors see this writing and mistakenly assume it is the name of the watchmaker, when in fact it is actually just describing the type of watch.

Here, then, **is** a list of commonly found foreign terms and what they actually mean:

Acier – steel or gunmetal [usually found on the case itself]

Aiguilles – Literally "needles" [or "hands"], this indicates which keyhole is for setting the time.

Ancre – indicates the watch has a lever escapement.

Balancier – the balance wheel

Balancier Compensateur – a compensated balance [i.e., one with little timing screws set along the edges]

Brevet – patented [usually followed by a patent number].

Chaux de Fonds – A Swiss town famous for watchmaking, part of the Neuchâtel region.

Chaton – jewel setting.

Cuivre – copper or brass [usually found on a dust cover to indicate that it is not gold or silver like the rest of the case].

Echappement – escapement.

Echappement a Ancre – lever escapement.

Echappement a Cylindre – cylinder escapement.

Echappement a Ligne Droit – straight line lever escapement [as opposed to the English-style right angle lever escapement]

et CIE – "and Company" [usually follows a name and indicates that this is the company that made/sold the watch].

et Fils – "and son" or "and sons" [watchmaking was often a family business handed down from generation to generation].

Geneve – Geneva, Switzerland [a watchmaking city].

Huit Trous Joyaux – literally, "eight holes jeweled." The watch may actually have more than 8 total jewels, though.

Levees Visibles – Visible escapement [technically, it means that the pallets, which are part of a lever escapement, can be seen from the back of the watch movement without disassembling it].

Locle – another watchmaking town in Switzerland.

Neuchâtel – another watchmaking region in Switzerland.

Remontoir – Keyless winding [technically, a remontoir is a small spiral spring, continually wound by the mainspring, which provides constant force to the escapement. However, this term is often used on low to medium grade antique Swiss watches simply to mean that the watch features the "new" stem winding feature].

Rubis – jewels [literally "rubies"]

Spiral Breguet – A type of hairspring [technically it describes a type of design of a part of the hairspring -- the overcoil -- but the important thing is that this describes the hairspring and **not** the watch or its maker].

So, for example, a watch that has the following engraved on the **dust cover**:

ANCRE a Ligne Droit SPIRAL BREGUET

Huit Trous Joyaux Remontoir

Bautte et Fils GENEVE

would be a watch with a straight line lever escapement, a spiral Breguet hairspring, at least 8 jewels, is stem wound, and which was made [or just sold] by Bautte and Sons of Geneva, Switzerland.

Chapter 13.   Gold or Just Gold-Filled?

For obvious reasons, it's important to know whether your watch is in a solid gold case or whether it is merely gold-filled or gold plated ["gold-filled" consists of a base metal such as brass sandwiched between two thin layers of gold]. The only way to be absolutely sure whether your watch case is solid gold, of course, is to take it to a competent and reputable jeweler and have it tested. But many watch cases are marked in such a way that you can usually figure it out if you know what to look for. Here are some pointers:

If the case is **solid gold**, it will often have a mark stating the gold content, such as "14K" or "18K". Some [especially early American] case makers unscrupulously marked gold-filled cases as "14K" or "18K", supposedly indicating that the cases were 14 or 18-karat **gold-filled**, so it is always best if the case also says something like "Warranted US Assay" after the karat marking. Again, when in doubt, have it professionally tested.

Some, especially European, watches express the gold content as a decimal. Pure gold is 24K, so a 18K watch would have "0.750" stamped on it and a 14K watch would have "0.585" stamped on it.

If a watch is only **gold-filled** it will often state that it is such. "**Rolled gold**" and "**rolled gold plate**" are similar terms that mean it is not solid gold. Note that a "14K Gold Filled" case is still just gold-filled.

A **gold-filled** case will often state how many years the gold is warranted to wear. Any time you see a period of years ["Guaranteed 20 years, "Warranted 10 years," etc.] you can be sure the case is gold-filled and NOT solid gold. Keep in mind that an unusually heavy gold-filled case can sometimes produce a false reading when tested for gold content, and a solid gold case will NEVER be marked with a number of years it is warranted to wear. It is not uncommon to see a case marked "warranted 25 years" that is being sold as "solid gold" by a [hopefully] ignorant seller, and an informed buyer needs to be aware what he or she is actually buying.

Chapter 14.   "Real" Silver vs. Fake

Although silver isn't nearly as valuable as gold, it's still nice to know if your watch is in a silver case or just a silver-colored case. Watch cases made in Europe were often stamped with hallmarks to guarantee that they were silver, but this was not the case [no pun intended] in the U.S. And to make matters worse, not only were there a number of types of silver, some companies actually made up misleading names for their non silver cases. Again, the only way to be absolutely sure is to take your watch to a competent and reputable jeweler and have it tested, but many watch cases are marked in such a way that you can usually figure it out if you know what to look for. Here are some pointers:

If the case has a decimal number on it, such as "**0.800**," "**0.925**" or "**0.935**," it is probably silver. These numbers represent the purity of the silver, with "1" being pure silver.

If the case is marked "**Sterling**," this indicates that it is high grade silver [at least **0.925** pure].

"Fine silver" usually refers to **0.995** pure silver.

If the case is marked "**Coin Silver**" it is still real silver, but of a lesser grade than sterling. In Europe, "coin silver" usually meant **0.800 pure**, whereas in the U.S. it generally meant **0.900** pure.

The following are trade names for silver colored alloys which do not actually contain any silver: "**Silveroid**," "**Silverine**," "**Silveride**," "**Nickel Silver**" and "**Oresilver**" [these last two are particularly sneaky, since they sound like they are a silver alloy of some sort or simply low grade silver]. Also, beware of cases marked "Alaskan Silver," "German Silver," etc.

Chapter 15.   Asking the "Experts" for Information about Your Watch

Hardly a day goes by that I don't get e-mail from somebody wanting my help in identifying an old pocket watch that they just bought or inherited. Often the person includes a ton of detail about the watch, but at the same time fails to give me the information I actually need to help them. So, if you're thinking of writing to an "expert" for help with identifying your watch, here are some basic pointers.

In general, keep in mind that the watch **movement** is the key part of the watch – not the dial, not the case, not the hands. The case, dial and hands may affect the watch's **value**, but they don't help in **identifying** it.

Whenever possible, include a picture of the watch. And be sure to include a clear one of the **movement**.

Include EVERYTHING that is written on the watch **movement**. For American-made watches, the serial number is crucially important. And remember – the serial number of the watch will be written on the actual **movement** and NOT the case. Unless you are specifically trying to find out information on a case, such as whether it is gold, gold-filled, silver, etc., nothing written on the case will be much help in identifying the watch. The only real exception is European watches, which may have important information written on the **dust cover** instead of the movement.

Most pocket watches have a separate dial for the second hand located near the 6. You don't need to mention this. What *would* be interesting, though, is if there were no second hand, or if the second hand were in the center, or if there were any additional dials [day/date, wind indicator, etc.]

Chapter 16. Most Common American Watch Companies

American Waltham Watch Company (Waltham, MA. 1851-1957)

Also commonly referred to as the "Waltham Watch Company," the American Waltham Watch Company was the first company to mass produce watches in America and is generally considered to be the most important American watch company. The history of the company is a little complicated, but it all started in 1850 when Edward Howard, David Davis and Aaron Dennison got together in Roxbury, Massachusetts, and decided to start their own watch company. They formed the "American Horologue Company" in 1851 and 17 prototype watches were produced in 1852 with "Howard, Davis & Dennison" engraved on the movements. The name of the company was then changed to the "Warren Mfg. Co.", and the next 26 or so watches produced bore the name "Warren" on their movements. The name was officially changed to the "Boston Watch Company" in 1853, and in 1854 a factory was built in **Waltham**, Massachusetts. The founders of the company certainly knew how to make great watches, but weren't so hot at managing money, and the Boston Watch Company failed in 1857. The story doesn't end there, though! The defunct company was sold at a sheriff's auction to a man named Royal Robbins, and he reorganized the company and renamed it the "Appleton, Tracy & Co." In 1859 the Appleton, Tracy & Co. merged with another company called the Waltham Improvement Company, and "The American Watch Company" was born. Soon after that, the company name was changed to "The American Waltham Watch Co.," and in later years the watches simply bore the name "Waltham." Note that The American Waltham Watch Company bears no relation whatsoever to the similarly named "U. S. Watch Co. of Waltham" which was founded in 1884.

Over 35 million Waltham watches were produced during the company's long history, and many of them still exist today. Although they made many low and medium grade watches to suit the needs of the existing markets, Waltham also produced watches of exceedingly high quality. They also probably produced more **types** of watches than any other American company, including railroad watches, chronographs, repeating watches and deck watches. Early Waltham watches with low serial numbers are especially prized by many collectors.

Ball Watch Company (Cleveland, OH 1879-1969)

Webb C. Ball of Cleveland, Ohio, was the general time inspector for a large chunk of the railroads in the late 1800's and early 1900's. It was Ball who was originally commissioned by certain railroad officials to develop the standards for railroad approved watches. The Ball Watch Company didn't produce any watches itself, but instead had high-grade watches manufactured by other companies made to Ball's specifications and the company literally placed its stamp of approval on them and marketed them under the Ball name. Ball watches were made primarily by Waltham and Hamilton, although there were also a small number made by Aurora, Elgin, Illinois, Hampden and Howard. There were also some Swiss-made Ball watches, but these are not as prized by railroad watch collectors as the American models. One interesting note is that Ball was not a fan of highly jeweled watches, feeling that anything beyond 17 or 19 jewels was unnecessary, although he did later market 21 and 23 jewels watches as the market demanded them.

Elgin Watch Company (Elgin, IL 1864-1964)

Formed in 1864 as the National Watch Company of Elgin, Illinois, the company officially changed its name to the "Elgin National Watch Company" in 1874. Some of the founders of the company, including P. S. Bartlett, had previously worked for the Waltham Watch Company. With the exception of the so-called "dollar" watches, Elgin made more pocket watches than any other single watch company – over 55 million of them – and made them in all sizes and grades.

Hamilton Watch Company (Lancaster, PA 1892-Present)

Much like the American Waltham Watch Company before it, the Hamilton Watch Company evolved over a period of years. In 1874, the Adams & Perry Watch Manufacturing Company was formed, and the first watch was produced in 1876. By 1877, the company had turned into the Lancaster Watch Company. In 1886, the company was bought out by a gentleman named Abram Bitner who renamed it the "Keystone Standard Watch Company." The business was then sold to the Hamilton Watch Company in 1891, and Hamilton officially sold its first watch in 1893.

Hamilton produced many fine pocket watches of all sizes and grades, and some of their models were considered the main "workhorses" of the railroad. In 1941, they won the contract from the U.S. government to produce marine chronometers, and these are highly prized today as some of the finest timepieces ever made. Hamilton eventually became part of a Swiss watch conglomerate, and the last American-made Hamilton was produced in about 1969.

Hampden Watch Company (Springfield, MA/Canton, OH 1877- 1930)

In 1877 John C. Deuber, formerly the owner of a watch case company, bought a controlling interest in the New York Watch Mfg. Co. [located, despite its name, in Springfield, Massachusetts] and renamed it the Hampden Watch Company. In 1889 Mr. Deuber relocated the company to Canton, Ohio, where it remained until being bought out by a Russian company in 1930. Hampden made a wide variety of pocket watches of all sizes and grades, and they were the first American company to produce a 23 jewel watch in 1894. Production records for Hampden are sketchy at best, and it's not uncommon to find a model or grade which is not mentioned in any of the standard price guides.

E. Howard & Company (Boston, MA 1879-1903)

Edward Howard was one of the three original founders of the company that became the American Waltham Watch Company. When the original company failed in 1857, Mr. Howard was able to secure all the unfinished movements and started his own company with Charles Rice in 1858. At first, this new company of "Howard & Rice" merely finished the leftover watches and placed its name on them, but the company soon began to produce its own, completely different, watches under the name "E. Howard & Co." Howard introduced many innovations to American watchmaking, and may have been the first to produce stem wound watches in America. Because Howard made their watches completely different from those produced by other companies, they wouldn't fit inside standard cases and they had to have cases specially made for their watches. As a result, it is very common to see old Howard watches without a case, since replacements were very hard to come by if the original case was damaged or melted down for its gold value. As with early Walthams, early Howards are especially prized by collectors due to their historical significance.

E. Howard Watch Co. [Keystone] (Jersey City, NJ 1902-1930)

In 1902 the Howard **name** was purchased by the **Keystone Watch Case Company**. The watches that were produced by Keystone under this name were completely different from the earlier Howards. Nevertheless, many fine watches were made, including some exceedingly high grade railroad watches.

Illinois Watch Company (Springfield, IL 1869-1927)

Organized in 1869, Illinois made many low, medium and high grade watches before being sold to the Hamilton Watch Company in 1927. They are especially known for the large number of railroad grade and railroad approved watches they produced, including the Bunn Special, the Sangamo Special and the Santa Fe Special. Illinois also used more names on their watches than any other company, including names of companies which simply sold the watches, such as "Burlington Watch Co." and "Washington Watch Co."

Other Common American Watch Companies

Aurora Watch Co. (Aurora, IL 1883-1892)

Columbus Watch Co. (Columbus, OH 1874-1903)

Ingersoll (New York, NY 1892-1922)

Ingraham (Bristol, CT 1912-1968)

New England Watch Co. (Waterbury, CT 1898-1914)

New York Standard Watch Co. (Jersey City, NJ 1885- 1929)

Peoria Watch Co. (Peoria, IL 1885-1895)

Rockford Watch Co. (Rockford, IL 1873-1915)

South Bend Watch Co. (South Bend, IN 1903-1929)

Seth Thomas Watch Co. (Thomaston, CT 1883-1915)

Trenton Watch Co. (Trenton, NJ 1885-1908)

United States Watch Co. (Marion, NJ 1865-1877)

U.S. Watch Co. of Waltham (Waltham, MA 1884-1905)

Waterbury Watch Co. (Waterbury, CT 1880-1898)

Chapter 17. How Old Is My Watch?

With many old pocket watches, it is difficult or even impossible to determine the exact date of production. In many cases, especially with lower grade European watches that were marketed under a variety of names, it is often impossible to even determine who the true manufacturer is. Many times, you have to rely solely on experience, comparing known examples to a watch at hand.

Most major American watch companies, on the other hand, kept relatively detailed production records, and it is often possible to determine the approximate date of an American made watch based solely on the serial number engraved on its **movement** (note that cases were made separately, often by entirely different companies, and on the serial number on the movement can be used to date a watch). In this chapter, I list approximate production dates based on serial number ranges for some of the more common American watch companies.

As for why the production dates are often only approximate, even for American companies that kept records, keep in mind that many companies stamped watch parts with serial numbers well in advance of the watch actually being assembled and sold. In addition, some companies reserved blocks of serial numbers in advance for certain models and grades, meaning that the serial numbers may not always be in strict chronological order. For these reasons, the actual date a particular watch left the factory may vary by as much as a couple of years from the date listed in the following tables.

To use the tables below, first determine the manufacturer of your watch. If it is one of the manufacturers listed below, locate the serial number on the watch's **movement** (not the outer case). Then, in the appropriate table, locate the closest serial number that is higher than your watch's serial number and look to the column immediately to the right to determine the approximate date. For example, if you had an American Waltham watch with a serial number of 7427102, you could determine that it's approximate date of production was 1896 as follows:

Serial No.	Date
7,450,000	1896

American Waltham

Serial No.	Date	Serial No.	Date	Serial No.	Date	Serial No.	Date	Serial No.	Date
50	1852	730,000	1874	7,450,000	1896	21,800,000	1918	30,250,000	1940
400	1853	810,000	1875	8,100,000	1897	22,500,000	1919	30,750,000	1941
1,000	1854	910,000	1876	8,400,000	1898	23,400,000	1920	31,050,000	1942
2,500	1855	1,000,000	1877	9,000,000	1899	23,900,000	1921	31,400,000	1943
4,000	1856	1,150,000	1878	9,500,000	1900	24,100,000	1922	31,700,000	1944
6,000	1857	1,350,000	1879	10,200,000	1901	24,300,000	1923	32,100,000	1945
10,000	1858	1,500,000	1880	11,100,000	1902	24,550,000	1924	32,350,000	1946
15,000	1859	1,670,000	1881	12,100,000	1903	24,800,000	1925	32,750,000	1947
20,000	1860	1,835,000	1882	13,500,000	1904	25,200,000	1926	33,100,000	1948
30,000	1861	2,000,000	1883	14,300,000	1905	26,100,000	1927	33,500,000	1949
45,000	1862	2,350,000	1884	14,700,000	1906	26,400,000	1928	33,560,000	1950
65,000	1863	2,650,000	1885	15,500,000	1907	26,900,000	1929	33,600,000	1951
110,000	1864	3,000,000	1886	16,400,000	1908	27,100,000	1930	33,700,000	1952
180,000	1865	3,400,000	1887	17,600,000	1909	27,300,000	1931	33,800,000	1953
260,000	1866	3,800,000	1888	17,900,000	1910	27,550,000	1932	34,100,000	1954
330,000	1867	4,200,000	1889	18,100,000	1911	27,750,000	1933	34,450,000	1955
410,000	1868	4,700,000	1890	18,200,000	1912	28,100,000	1934	34,700,000	1956
460,000	1869	5,200,000	1891	18,900,000	1913	28,600,000	1935	35,000,000	1957
500,000	1870	5,800,000	1892	19,500,000	1914	29,100,000	1936		
540,000	1871	6,300,000	1893	20,000,000	1915	29,400,000	1937		
590,000	1872	6,700,000	1894	20,500,000	1916	29,750,000	1938		
680,000	1873	7,100,000	1895	20,900,000	1917	30,050,000	1939		

Hamilton Watch Co.

Serial No.	Date	Serial No.	Date	Serial No.	Date	Serial No.	Date	Serial No.	Date
2,000	1893	1,050,500	1910	2,250,000	1927	C41,000	1942	C495,000	1959
5,000	1894	1,290,500	1911	2,300,000	1928	C75,000	1943	C510,000	1960
10,000	1895	1,331,000	1912	2,350,000	1929	C85,000	1944	C511,000	1961
14.000	1896	1,370,000	1913	2,400,000	1930	C115,000	1945	C513,000	1962
20,000	1897	1,410,500	1914	2,450,000	1931	C145,000	1946	C515,000	1963
30,000	1898	1,450,500	1915	2,500,000	1932	C169,000	1947	C517,000	1964
40,000	1899	1,517,000	1916	2,600,000	1933	C210,000	1948	C519,000	1965
50,000	1900	1,580,000	1917	2,700,000	1934	C250,000	1949	C521,000	1966
90,000	1901	1,650,000	1918	2,800,000	1935	C290,000	1950	C523,000	1967
150,000	1902	1,700,000	1919	2,900,000	1936	C325,000	1951	C525,000	1968
260,000	1903	1,790,000	1920	3,000,000	1937	C345,000	1952	C529,169	1969

Serial No.	Date	Serial No.	Date	Serial No.	Date	Serial No.	Date	Serial No.	Date
340,000	1904	1,860,000	1921	3,200,000	1938	C365,000	1953		
425,000	1905	1,900,000	1922	3,400,000	1939	C396,300	1954		
590,000	1906	1,950,000	1923	3,600,000	1940	C416,000	1955		
756,000	1907	2,000,000	1924	3,800,000	1941	C435,000	1956		
921,000	1908	2,100,000	1925	4,025,000	1942	C455,000	1957		
1,087,000	1909	2,200,000	1926	C11,000	1941	C475,000	1958		

Elgin

Serial No.	Date	Serial No.	Date	Serial No.	Date	Serial No.	Date	Serial No.	Date
101	1867	1,850,000	1885	10,100,000	1903	24,000,000	1921	38,200,000	1939
31,000	1868	2,000,000	1886	11,000,000	1904	25,000,000	1922	39,100,000	1940
71,000	1869	2,550,000	1887	12,100,000	1905	26,000,000	1923	40,200,000	1941
101,000	1870	3,000,000	1888	12,500,000	1906	27,000,000	1924	41,100,000	1942
126,000	1871	3,550,000	1889	13,100,000	1907	28,000,000	1925	42,200,000	1943
152,000	1872	4,000,000	1890	13,550,000	1908	29,000,000	1926	42,600,000	1944
176,000	1873	4,400,000	1891	14,100,000	1909	30,000,000	1927	43,200,000	1945
210,000	1874	4,890,000	1892	15,100,000	1910	32, 000,000	1928	44,000,000	1946
310,000	1875	5,000,000	1893	16,000,000	1911	33,000,000	1929	45,000,000	1947
410,000	1876	5,500,000	1894	17,000,000	1912	33,300,000	1930	46,000,000	1948
510,000	1877	6,000,000	1895	17,550,000	1913	33,500,000	1931	47,000,000	1949
552,000	1878	6,550,000	1896	18,000,000	1914	33,700,000	1932	48,000,000	1950
601,000	1879	7,000,000	1897	18,500,000	1915	34,000,000	1933	50,000,000	1951
701,000	1880	7,550,000	1898	19,000,000	1916	35, 000,000	1934	52,000,000	1952
801,000	1881	8,100,000	1899	20,000,000	1917	35,500,000	1935	53,300,000	1953
1,000,000	1882	9,100,000	1900	21,000,000	1918	36,200,000	1936	54,000,000	1954
1,440,000	1883	9,350,000	1901	22,000,000	1919	37,000,000	1937	54,500,000	1955
1,650,000	1884	9,755,000	1902	23,000,000	1920	37,900,000	1938	55,000,000	1956

Hampden

Serial No.	Date	Serial No.	Date	Serial No.	Date	Serial No.	Date	Serial No.	Date
60,000	1877	450,000	1887	1,000,000	1897	2,280,000	1907	3,560,000	1917
91,000	1878	500,000	1888	1,128,000	1898	2,408,000	1908	3,680,000	1918
122,000	1879	555,500	1889	1,256,000	1899	2,536,000	1909	3,816,000	1919
153,000	1880	611,000	1890	1,384,000	1900	2,664,000	1910	3,944,000	1920
184,000	1881	666,500	1891	1,512,000	1901	2,792,000	1911	4,072,000	1921
215,000	1882	722,000	1892	1,642,000	1902	2,920,000	1912	4,200,000	1922

Serial No.	Date	Serial No.	Date	Serial No.	Date	Serial No.	Date	Serial No.	Date
250,000	1883	775,000	1893	1,768,000	1903	3,046,000	1913	4,400,000	1923
300,000	1884	833,000	1894	1,896,000	1904	3,176,000	1914	4,600,000	1924
350,000	1885	888,500	1895	2,024,000	1905	3,304,000	1915		
400,000	1886	944,000	1896	2,152,000	1906	3,432,000	1916		

Illinois

Serial No.	Date	Serial No.	Date	Serial No.	Date	Serial No.	Date	Serial No.	Date
5,000	1872	550,000	1885	1,400,000	1898	2,314,000	1911	4,492,501	1924
20,000	1873	600,000	1886	1,450,000	1899	2,408,000	1912	4,547,001	1925
50,000	1874	700,000	1887	1,500,000	1900	2,502,000	1913	4,700,000	1926
75,000	1875	800,000	1888	1,550,000	1901	2,596,000	1914	4,850,000	1927
100,000	1876	900,000	1889	1,600,000	1902	2,689,101	1915	5,100,000	1928
145,000	1877	1,000,000	1890	1,650,000	1903	2,873,000	1916	5,200,000	1929
210,000	1878	1,075,000	1891	1,700,000	1904	3,057,000	1917	5,300,000	1930
250,000	1879	1,120,000	1892	1,749,801	1905	3,241,000	1918	5,400,000	1931
300,000	1880	1,165,000	1893	1,844,000	1906	3,425,000	1919	5,500,000	1932
350,000	1881	1,210,000	1894	1,938,000	1907	3,609,000	1920		
400,000	1882	1,255,000	1895	2,032,000	1908	3,793,000	1921		
450,000	1883	1,300,001	1896	2,126,000	1909	3,977,000	1922		
500,000	1884	1,350,000	1897	2,220,000	1910	4,166,801	1923		

Chapter 18.   Other Sources of Information

O.K., now that you can "talk the talk," what's next? Well, if you're serious about being a pocket watch collector, here are some good sources of invaluable information that will help you continue what is sure to be a fascinating and fun-filled journey!

Complete Price Guide to Watches [, Engle and Gilbert] – At over 1000 pages, this book is a veritable encyclopedia of useful general information in addition to being a great overall guide to what various watches are worth on today's market. A new edition is published each year, with 2017 seeing the release of No. 27. Look for it at your local bookstore, or contact the publisher at Collector Books, P.O. Box 3009, 5801 Kentucky Dam Road, KY 42001.

Join the NAWCC – The National Association of Watch and Clock Collectors exists to promote the hobbies of watch and clock collecting. For a small membership fee, members receive the regularly published NAWCC Bulletin, which is full of informative articles, as well as the NAWCC Mart, which allows members to buy, sell and trade with other members. Membership also allows you to attend regularly scheduled meetings in your local area where you can meet fellow enthusiasts, talk about the hobby and buy, sell and trade face to face with other collectors. For more information, visit the official NAWCC Website at www.nawcc.org.

Made in the USA
Columbia, SC
10 December 2019